From the Back of a Donkey

Journey of a Lifetime
Second Edition

Light Bringer Publishing
& Studio, LLC.

From the Back of a Donkey

Journey of a Lifetime

Second Edition

NANCY ELAINE HARTMAN MINOR

Nancy Elaine Hartman Minor
COPYRIGHT © 2009 -2023
From the Back of a Donkey - Journey of a
Lifetime - Second Edition

Editor: Elizabeth Maynard Charle, Reedsy
Marketplace Professional

Guest Content Editors: Rev. David L. Carey
Rev. Mary Beth Brocklebank

Foreword by: Dr. Thomas P. Kiley

Printed in the USA
First Printing December 2022

Library of Congress Control Number:
2023917142

ISBN: 979-8-9874670-2-2
Digital online epub ISBN: 979-8-9874670-3-9

Published by:
Light Bringer Publishing and Studio, LLC. Elkton,
MD. 21921
www.lightbringerpublishingstudio.com

Scripture references appear at the end of each chapter:

Unless otherwise stated, all scriptural references and paraphrase are from the King James Version (KJV) of the Bible. (Public Domain, USA)

BSB
The Holy Bible, Berean Standard Bible, BSB is produced in cooperation with Bible Hub, Discovery Bible, OpenBible.com, and the Berean Bible Translation Committee. This text of God's Word was officially dedicated to the public domain April 30, 2023.

Free resources and databases are available at BereanBible.com (FYI: It is also listed as the Berean Study Bible in the Bible Hub app.)

NASB
Scripture quotations taken from the (NASB ®) New American Standard Bible®, Copyright © 2020 by The Lockman Foundation.
Used by permission. All Rights Reserved.
www. lockman.org © 2020

NLT
Scripture quotations marked (NLT) are taken from the Holy Bible, New Living Translation, copyright ©1996, 2004, 2015 by Tyndale House Foundation. Used by permission of Tyndale

ACKNOWLEDGEMENTS

Foreword by: Rev. Dr. Thomas P. Kiley
Founder of Wellspring Christian Center, Rutland, Vt.
Founder and Pastor of Abundant Waters of Life
Church, Broken Arrow, OK.

Editorial Contributions by: Apostle David
Carey, for reviewing, proofreading, and making
many invaluable suggestions, from content, to
syntax, to graphic design advice.

Apostle David Carey, author of "Now Elijah!"
along with his wife Nancy Carey, is the founder
of Word of Life Christian Center, Newark, DE.
He is the cofounder of the Delaware Coalition
of Apostles, a long-standing member of the
International Coalition of Apostolic Leaders, and
on the Advisory Board for the United States
Coalition of Apostolic Leaders.

Additional proofreading and suggestions by:
Rev. Mary Beth Brocklebank, B.S., MDiv,
Daughters for Zion (CUFI) Delaware State
Director, Israel Advocate and Israel Tour Host

Final Editing by: Elizabeth Maynard Charle,
Reedsy Marketplace Professional

Information of second century temple crafts by: Suri Provisor, Weaver/Ancient Crafts Specialist, Director and teacher at Kaduma, located in Shilo, Israel (Ancient Shiloh)

Front book cover by: Siriusartss69 via Fiverr.com

Back cover design: composite of a picture of Israel countryside from Pixaby.com (free use) plus a portion of a corresponding design by Siriusartss69 to match the front cover. Photoshop editing by the author.

Cover formatting by: Arcanic Media

Inside formatting done using InDesign by: Bala Subramanian of Fiverr.com and Elizabeth Maynard Charle of Reedsy.com

Illustrations:
"Carved Wooden Box," photo of actual gift that was given to the author on a mission trip to Belarus.

"Mary at the Loom" (based on information provided by Suri Provisor, Weaver/Ancient Crafts Specialist, Shilo Israel) and "Brown Donkey Loaded for Travel" by Khairin Nisa via Siriusartss69 at Fiverr.com

Christmas Crib by "falco" Pixaby user_id:81448

A rendition of Mary and Joseph hunting for lodging in Bethlehem free usage https://pixabay.com/photos/christmas-crib-christmas-party-2605870/

Map Illustration of Ancient Israel by Jeff Jacobs user_id:7438739 on Pixaby free usage https://pixabay.com/illustrations/map- jerusalem-israel-bible-6508505/

Photography: Mary Praying at the Manger by Susan M. Santa Maria via Dreamstime. Regular license.

DEDICATION

I dedicate this book to
My Heavenly Father
Who has bestowed
"the gift of words" upon me,
and to
The Holy Spirit, who guided
me as I wrote,
And to My Lord and
Savior Jesus Christ,
To Whom
I owe my life and
All of my praise.
Accept these pages as my
Offering of Worship
To You.

Table of Contents

IN PRAISE OF. . .

From the Back of a Donkey
~Journey of a Lifetime~
Nancy Elaine Hartman Minor

Praise be to God for our author, sister and Reverend, Nancy Elaine Hartman Minor. Skillfully, she narrates in this beautiful book the story of the birth of Jesus. *From the Back of a Donkey: Journey of a Lifetime* is the gospel in miniature form. From the Annunciation by the angel, to the birth of Jesus, to the appearance of the angels' announcement to the shepherds, these divine events describe the unfolding of the first Christmas.

It is a beautiful retelling and rediscovery as our sister does not just provide the readers an opportunity to read words. Reflective of her "intentional-about-being-relational" spirit, she invites readers to embrace the miraculous truth of Christ's appearing, while reflecting and journaling our response to this colorful and true narrative that warms the heart and soul.

After all that the world has witnessed, in the aftermath of a global pandemic and other social challenges, there has never been so great a time to hear again, this glorious birth and salvation story. Praise be to God for her evangelistic heart as she narrates new revelations and joys of finding our Savior and Lord, again and again.

This would be a welcome workbook for a conference or a personal devotional. Secure your copy and accept the invitation to read, journal, and to be blessed with, *From the Back of a Donkey: Journey of a Lifetime!*

Rev. Dr. Frederick T. Faison
Lincoln University of Pennsylvania
Chaplain and Associate Vice President of Health and Wellness

This unique devotional offers fresh insights to a familiar story. Nancy's detailed personal research informs the reader, while her reflection questions stir the reader's own heart-journey.

This beloved story changed history. Reading it from Mary's perspective will bless your life.

Rev. Mary Beth Brocklebank, B.S., MDiv, Daughters for Zion (CUFI) Delaware State Director, Israel Advocate and Israel Tour Host

This book, *From the Back of a Donkey - Journey of a Lifetime*, is an excellent, yet simple, piece of creativity. The writer employs graphic imagery that paints a picture and brings to life the simplistic grassroots behind the factual advent of Jesus' birth. The creativity brings a dimension of spiritual understanding to the experience of young Mary chosen by God to be the mother of our Lord Jesus. The Bible depicts Mary as a thoughtful woman who kept many profound experiences to herself.

Hence, here we read her diary and have a glimpse of her inner contemplation. By this, we can also appreciate her devotion to God and her faith in the One who is able to do the impossible: a young virgin actually became pregnant and gave birth to a sacred Son!

This gentle book also prods us on, to go on trusting and believing the unfailing Eternal Father who does not fail to keep His word.

Dr. Olufunso Joseph Omidiran, LivingSword
Apostolic Network Inc., Nigeria.

A private note to the author:

I just finished reading the book! It is such an
amazing creative piece of literature put together
through you by the help of the Holy Spirit.
May the Lord renew your strength and creative
genius day by day. Amen.

*From the Back of a Donkey - the Journey of a
Lifetime* transports the reader into the biblical
story of the Virgin Mary giving birth to our Lord
and Savior, Jesus Christ. Nancy's "first-hand"
account of Mary's journey brings the story to
life and captures the reader's heart.

After reading this narrative, I have a
new appreciation of what Mary may have
experienced before Jesus' birth. Nancy's fresh
perspective brings to life a familiar story and
incites a new love in the reader's heart.

Elizabeth Maynard Charle
Editor and Author

Comments from the blog series by the same name:

Opal said...

My friend, thank you, thank you, thank you! Oh, what a joy to read! I felt like I was transported far away from my surroundings and was sitting with Mary, listening to her heart.

You have opened up possibilities in the Scriptures that I had never considered before. You've made it all come alive in a fresh, new way. I am SEEING the Scriptures like I've never seen them before. And realizing, these people had lives. Day to day lives that were intersected with God. It's amazing. Thank you.

Keep writing! I believe God is going to give you even greater access to write more along these lines.

Love, Opal

Raymonda said...

My precious, multi-gifted, sweet friend,

I have waited until today [Christmas Day] to "read" this last part. I just didn't want it to "end," and have savored every little morsel.

I had to stop several times during different parts...tears were streaming down my face. It is all so beautiful and "believable" and pure...

The whole journey was almost like truly being there, and being there from a new vantage point I'd never considered...

Abba has MANY, MANY more portions of His Life-filled, Living WORD He will have you share, Nancy... and, of a certainty, to be published, in more than one form...

Thank you, Nancy... It came from such a tender part of His Great Heart. Love you!

Raymonda

APPRECIATION

I wish to say thank you to my dear friends Pastor Tom Kiley and his late wife, Pastor Peggy Ann. Ours is a God-connection for which I am eternally grateful. You have steadfastly believed in me and encouraged me through the years. Thank you for writing the foreword!

A special thank you to my good friend, Apostle David Carey, Founder of Word of Life Christian Center in Newark, Delaware, and author of *Now Elijah* for graciously answering a myriad of questions and sharing his biblical knowledge and tenured perspective with me, turning a keen eye to the manuscript.

Thank you to my friend, Mary Beth Brocklebank, for providing invaluable insight and for connecting me with Suri Provisor, Weaver/Ancient Crafts Specialist, located in Shilo, Israel, who gave detailed information regarding second century temple looms and spindles in use then. Thank you Suri!

Thank you to Elizabeth Maynard Charle, from Reedsy, for undertaking to be my copy editor on short notice.

Elizabeth, you took my manuscript and went over it with a fine tooth comb. Thank you for all your suggestions, expertise, and patience! You made it shine, and made sure it's a quality piece that honors God in every facet.

Thank you to my friend and colleague, Rev. Dr. Frederick Faison, Chaplain of Mary Dod Brown Chapel, on the Lincoln University Campus. Thank you for taking time out of your very busy schedule to read the manuscript and write such an effusive review.

A special mention to my dear friend, adopted nephew, former colleague, and Mr. Maryland U.S. United 2023, Jonathan Harris, aka "Author Jon," who has shared his own writing journeys of three plus books and multiple resources with me, and much encouragement. Thank you.

I have had the blessing of several friends who have encouraged me over the years, particularly in regards to my writing gift. Jackie Toliver and Raymonda Wise, my two besties, thank you! Also to Karen Sattem for your ever-ready prayers and friendship. To all of you who I haven't mentioned specifically – hugs and a big thank you!

Love to my family, my darling husband Tom, (for allowing me uninterrupted hours at my computer), and our sons and their families.

I must acknowledge my beloved "daughter-in-love," Eni, who shared her own manuscript with me, Masango y el Sendero de la Sombra. It was so powerful, I cried. Not only is it now published, but also includes many series of lessons to go with it. Eni, you lit a fire under me to get to work and get my book completed! Thank you for your love and trust in sharing your tender heart with me.

To my little sister, Julie: God heard my prayer at six years old, when I asked Him to send me a baby sister to love. Never mind the doctor's negative reports that Mom would not be able to conceive again. You were a huge albeit, happy surprise to Mom and Dad, but no surprise to me, just a joyous answer to that prayer when I had asked Him for you. I love you always!

Love and thank you to my adopted Dad, Pastor Rusty Bowles of Garland, Texas, for your love and prayers, and to the church family there, for lovingly welcoming me. Special hi to my "sister" Yajaira!

To all my church family in multiple states, you make life all the richer. Please know that you are such a huge blessing, and I treasure our fellowship and times together.

My Dover family, you've been an integral part of my life and progress. I am so blessed that you are in my life. Thank you.

To Word of Life Christian Center in Newark, Delaware, thank you for your kindness and encouragement, and for opening the door to host a Book Club small group with my book!

To all my spiritual children scattered across the globe: I send love and prayers. Keep following Jesus and honoring Him with your lives.

Also a "shout out" to my twelfth grade English teacher, Mrs. Webster, at Princess Anne High School. You were tough, but caring, encouraging me to think for myself and draw my own conclusions from my lessons. Because of your insistence of six weeks of grammar, I can write a proper sentence! Thank you for being a teacher.

To my Dad: you left Earth too soon, Dad, but your loving, gentle, and listening heart made it easy for me to accept God as a loving father.

I have never forgotten your homily, "never judge a man until you've walked a mile in his moccasins."

(Your own special nod to our neighbors in the Native American Communities around us, where you were always welcomed.)

Look, your legacy lives on, Dad: The "miracle baby of Penn Street" that you and mom waited for, now writes about the biggest miracle of all! I love you and I display the Hartman name proudly as an author.

Last but not least, thank you Mom. You were always my greatest cheerleader. I know you are still cheering me on from Heaven. I love you.

Nancy

INTRODUCTION

What you are about to read was originally written as a five-part series on my blog, as a gift to my readership. I prayed and asked God to give me something special for Christmas of 2009. This is the result of that prayer. I was subsequently encouraged to turn it into a book.

It is my prayer that the Scriptures come alive to you, and that you are greatly blessed and your Christmas is enriched with new dimensions. Be blessed as you read.

In the first and second chapters of Luke's gospel, we have what is commonly called "The Christmas Story." I have taken my narrative from those pages.

I will begin with what Luke has written and then give what I was inspired to write as being from the perspective of this young girl named Mary, who submitted herself to the will of God.

Nancy

FOREWORD BY
REV. DR. THOMAS P. KILEY

Throughout my years of Bible reading and studies, I have always been captivated by the ordinary men and women I read about in the Bible. These were regular people like you and me, yet they allowed their lives to be changed forever, simply by believing God at His Word. Sometimes we seem to forget that they all went through the same challenges, temptations, doubts, and fears that we do. They set them all aside and were moved by a faith that changed the world!

Nancy has given us a wonderful portrayal of a young woman in the Bible named Mary. An ordinary woman doing ordinary things in an ordinary life. She had so many hopes, desires, plans, and responsibilities. That suddenly all changed when God intervened with a message – "You are chosen to be the mother of Jesus!"

It was her response of faith that changed the world forever! Nancy also augments the chapters of Mary's story with life-pondering questions for each of us to ask and meditate upon. It gives us the ability to tune into the supernatural around our daily, ordinary lives.

Nancy captures the person and humanity of this young woman, Mary, as she has to deal with the realities of her handling this supernatural event in a natural world and society.

You will be eager to follow Mary's story as each chapter unfolds and enjoy her personal conversations about each event.

THOMAS P. KILEY, PHD

Founder, Wellspring Christian Center, Rutland, Vt.

Founder and Pastor, Abundant Waters of Life Church, Broken Arrow, OK.

PREFACE

Long ago, before time existed, it was decided. After having a conversation with Himself, God determined that He wanted a family. The company of angels though seemingly perfect in our eyes, did not satisfy the longing in His heart.

Even Lucifer, the chief angel in charge of worship and commerce, turned out to be a huge disappointment. Not happy with his position, Lucifer plotted a coup. He actually managed to sway one third of the angelic hosts to turn against God and follow him. However, that only succeeded in getting him kicked out of heaven.[1]

When he fell from Heaven, it is believed by many, that it was to Earth where he created much calamity, chaos, and destruction.[2]

Thus, the Holy Spirit came to Earth and hovered over the waters above the face of the deep oceans, just as a mother hen broods, laying herself across her eggs until they hatch; staying close, watching and caring for first the eggs, and then over her chicks. He was waiting for God's command to begin creating [again].[3]

Then God spoke! Sending out His Word and the Holy Spirit went to work…[4]

Seas were strategically placed as God hollowed out the spaces with his hand in which the waters would occupy. Trees and grasses, shrubs and flowers, and birds and bees, and fish in the sea; every kind of creature you could imagine was created.[5]

It was good, and it was beautiful, but still, something was missing.

Then God set about gathering the dust of the ground from the surface of the Earth. As He gathered, can't you hear Him singing? Even as He worked forming, making, molding, and shaping a body, He was singing some mysterious melody.[6]

When everything was just the way that God wanted it, gently He blew into the lifeless form, and man became a living, breathing person. And God was happy.[7]

God walked and talked with Adam and took pleasure in him.[8] He could tell however, that the man He had created was lonely. Just as God had been longing for someone like Himself, and so He created Adam in his own image, now Adam longed for someone that was like himself, here on Earth. That was when God put the man to sleep.[9]

As Adam slept, God took from within Adam, drawing from his side certain traits, assets and qualities. He then skillfully and artfully created it into someone that was like Adam, but yet different. All of those qualities, characteristics and traits that He had taken from out of Adam, He put into Eve.[10] Eve became the missing piece that completed Adam perfectly. Together, He knew that they would reflect the beauty and glory of Himself.

God went out on His daily walk and presented her to Adam.

Adam was delighted and intrigued. When Adam saw her he breathed out, "Oh Ishah!"[11a] The two were inseparable and immensely happy, as they explored their garden paradise together, and eagerly awaited God's daily visits.[11b]

However, Lucifer was lurking around, watching, waiting and still plotting against God. He saw how much God loved these two created human beings, and he was enraged, filled with jealousy and bitter about being kicked out of heaven. He now hated all that God loved, especially Adam and Eve!

Now, although God had given everything to Adam and Eve, the devil came as a serpent snake, talking to Eve to sway her into believing that God was stingy and withholding the best blessing from her and Adam.

Adam looked on, listening with curiosity. Although Adam had been charged with protecting and keeping the garden, he did not stop the snake from speaking to Eve, even when the serpent tempted Eve to take a bite of the "Forbidden Fruit."

Instead, he watched to see what would happen, because after all, if God really was withholding something good from them, and now Eve was going to be brave enough to taste it, he wanted to see what exactly would happen to her.[12]

Sure enough, she ate some, and turned to her husband who was there with her. "Oh Adam, take a taste! It's sweet, and oh my goodness, the knowledge that I now have! I feel so different." She did not yet realize the knowledge of good and evil, the knowledge of lying, deceiving and how to cheat, and a myriad of other things were now implanted into her being.[13]

Now the devil had gained entrance to their minds and emotions because their connection with God was broken and their spirits were slowly withering, cut off from their life source.[14]

However, this was not a surprise to God. The Holy Spirit had pointed this out long before God created any of it: "If the angels who were created perfect beings, and designed to only obey and worship You, and yet a third of them malfunctioned, then it's certain that these humans You desire to create will fall far from the mark where You've placed them. Especially with all of the choices and freedoms that You are planning to give to them!"

Amazingly, Father God answered, "Yes I know they will. Therefore, 'we' must have a rescue plan in place, before I create them. I AM going to need a perfect sacrifice to redeem them and pay for the penalty of their sins." It was at this point the Son spoke and said, "I will go Father." Thus, the Son became "the lamb, slain before the foundations of the world."[15]

Then looking down through the portals of time, the setting was selected. And two special people along with some of their family, were also chosen to interact with the greatest rescue mission to save mankind that the world has ever seen![16]

In fulfilling that plan, God saw the heart of a young girl who was so devoted and sold out to God that she was willing to give up everything, even possibly the man that she loved, to surrender herself to this plan that was laid out in the heavens long ago before God created mankind.

Because even before they were created, God loved them both; the male and the female. He loved them, and had already devised good plans for them.[17]

Hence, the glory, majesty, splendor, and beauty of all that God is, embraced Mary. The Holy Spirit surrounded and enveloped her with His Loving Presence.

Thus, being covered in God's glory, the Son then confined Himself in the tiny space of Mary's womb, and God of the Universe became an embryo. An embryo![18]

As a result, Mary carried Him in her womb; He was her most precious cargo. Carrying Him within her on her donkey, I guess you could say that Mary (with Jesus in her womb) became His first donkey ride, reminiscent of how another donkey would one day carry this same precious cargo into Jerusalem.

With anticipation, Mary waited for the birth of her baby boy all the while knowing that He wasn't really hers since He was the long-awaited Messiah.

And, Joseph? Well in the beginning he … but I'll let Mary tell you. This is after all Mary's story.

Scriptures used in the Preface:

1.   Ezekiel 28

2.   Isaiah 14:9-17, Luke 10:18

3.   Genesis 1:2

4.   Genesis 1:3

5.   Genesis 1:9-12

6.   Genesis 1:26, Zephaniah. 3:17

7.   Genesis 1:27, Genesis 2:7 AMPC

8.   Revelation 4:11

9.   Genesis 2:18

10. Genesis 2:21 AMPC

11a. Genesis 2:23 Brown-Driver-Briggs Hebrew Concordance H802H802

11b. Genesis 2:22-25 AMPC

12. Genesis 3:1-5

13. Genesis 1:6-7

14. Genesis 8-13, Romans 5:12, Romans 6:23

15. Revelation 13:8

16. Luke 1:1-18, John 1:1-34 1 Peter 1:17-21 KJV

17. John 3:16-17, Jeremiah 29:11

18. Luke 1:30-33

SCRIPTURES

In the sixth month, God sent the angel
Gabriel to a town in Galilee called
Nazareth, to a virgin pledged in marriage
to a man named Joseph, who was of the
house of David. And the virgin's name was
Mary. The angel appeared to her and said,
"Greetings, you who are highly favored!
The Lord is with you!"

Mary was greatly troubled at his words
and wondered what kind of greeting this
might be. So the angel told her, "Do not be
afraid, Mary, for you have found favor with
God. Behold, you will conceive and give
birth to a son, and you are to give Him the
name Jesus. He will be great and will be
called the Son of the Most High. The Lord
God will give Him the throne of His father
David, and He will reign over the house
of Jacob forever. His kingdom will never
end!"

"How can this be," Mary asked the angel,
"since I am a virgin?"

The angel replied, "The Holy Spirit will come upon you, and the power of the Most High will overshadow you. So the Holy One to be born will be called the Son of God. Look, even Elizabeth your relative has conceived a son in her old age, and she who was called barren is in her sixth month. For no word from God will ever fail. For nothing will be impossible with God."

"I am the Lord's servant," Mary answered. "May it happen to me according to your Word." Then the angel left her.

Luke 1:26-38 Berean Study Bible

Scriptures

Now in those days a decree went out from Caesar Augustus that a census should be taken of the whole empire. This was the first census to take place while Quirinius was governor of Syria. And everyone went to his own town to register.

So Joseph also went up from Nazareth in Galilee to Judea, to the city of David called Bethlehem, since he was from the house and line of David. He went there to register with Mary, who was pledged to him in marriage and was expecting a child.

While they were there, the time came for her Child to be born. And she gave birth to her firstborn, a Son. She wrapped Him in swaddling cloths and laid Him in a manger, because there was no room for them in the inn.

Luke 2:1-7 Berean Study Bible

This then is
Mary's account of
"The Christmas Story"
as seen through her
eyes and told
from the back of her
donkey.

Chapter One

AN ORDINARY DAY

I can't believe my time is so near! What a strange year this has been. So much has happened! I remember the beginning of the year when Joseph finally got up the courage to propose! Of course, he didn't come right out and SAY it, but rather he asked me in a roundabout way. Carefully, the same way he carves his wood and makes his furniture. With loving thought and attention, putting his whole heart into it, but not speaking much.

"Mary," he announced to me, "I've given much thought to the future." I wondered, "Does that future include me, Joseph?" He went on, "I am no longer an apprentice, but I am now a full blown carpenter. My pieces are selling quite handsomely. Why just the other day Mrs. Ben-Jehozodak ordered several tables from me! I can see my little carpenter shop growing and my sons helping me in it."

I had to smile. He was sharing his dreams with me, without actually telling me that they included me. But where else is he going to get sons? My only other competition was that girl Dina. However, she told me that although Joseph was handsome and polite, he was so boring to her!

She confided in me, "He's always talking about the grain of the wood and stopping in the marketplace to examine other pieces of work and to ask questions like, 'How did they do this or that?'" I thought to myself, "Good! You keep thinking that way Dina, because Joseph is mine! And we are going to be married!" Yes, I know that the parents must arrange the marriage, but I just knew that somehow, God would order our steps to each other.[1] And He did just that and worked out all the details of the engagement!

Although, the beginning of that day was a bit strange, and I should have guessed that something was going on. You see, Mother came to me mid-morning and sent me to town to get some things for her; things that I knew we already had in the house! Plus, she requested some special preserve jam that could only be bought on the other side of town!

When I returned there was a sweet little gray donkey tied up in front of the house. I wondered if Abba (as I call my Dad) had bought some new animals. Upon entering with my bags, I found Joseph speaking earnestly with my parents.

They motioned for me to come near and announced, "Joseph has asked for your hand in marriage. What do you say to this request?" Of course, I said, "Yes!"

You see, I don't care that he is not exciting to others, or dashing around being the life of everyone's party. I love how he examines the wood, looking for hidden beauty that no one else sees.

I find it exciting how he sees past what is right in front of him to what can be, and sets out to make it happen, turning a block of wood into a beautiful piece of craftsmanship.

Speaking of which, that was one of his presents to me! A small beautifully carved and polished wooden chest lined with blue velvet, to keep all of my treasures in. And a necklace of some gorgeous carved wooden beads, along with a more traditional gold necklace and bracelet.

Then he asked us to come outside with him. He had already presented many gifts to my parents as a dowry.

Outside, he presented us with a small, slender olive sapling, saying, "May it flourish and bring forth much fruit, as a covenant between our families and a sign of God's peace and blessings upon us, even as Mary and I flourish as a couple."

Then, last of all, he presented me with Misha! Who is Misha? Remember that darling gray donkey I told you about, tied out front? She is mine!

I gently reached out my hand, and she extended her muzzle toward me so I could stroke her nose. She was soft as velvet. I fell in love with her immediately. I named her Misha, which means, "Who is like God?" for certainly there is no other like our God!

Obviously, Joseph stopped looking at his wood at some point long enough to look at me and saw that I could be the perfect, loving helpmate for him.

Just like God did in the beginning. He looked down and said, "Let us make man in 'Our' image."[2] God envisioned each of us, and planned out blessings for our lives[3] and all we have to do is draw close to Him and He will reveal Himself.

He promised, and He always keeps His promises![4] But that is how all this got started! I was drawing close to God and seeking Him. At first I would just think about the Scriptures we heard at the temple readings and praising God for His words.

But soon I found myself asking questions aloud and wondering about things as I went about my day-to-day chores. And really that is how it all started.

It was just another ordinary day and …

~to be continued.

What about your journey? What is your story? As we journey with Mary, how does it relate to your life? How and where has God shown up for you in your life?

Yes, He is there in your hard and sad times. But, how has He also shown Himself to you in your "ordinary" days? Like Mary, I believe that the more we see His hand in ordinary things and appreciate them, the more He can and will show us. Then, when some big trial comes along in our lives, we will be able to remember "how He saved us from the bear and lion,"[5] or just provided a surprise blessing to us. Be thinking of these questions and journal a few memorable moments of your own!

Dear Lord, thank You for looking past all the "non-descript" in my life and seeing the inner beauty that You have placed inside of me. Help me to develop that confidence that You really are making something beautiful out of my life, despite what I see right in front of me. I want to trust You more and draw closer day by day. Help me to see glimpses of You in and through the little things in my days. Glimpses of You in those that You put in my path, and teach me to look to what CAN BE, to see the beauty and wonder with the eyes of a child secure in the Father's Love, instead of just what I see with natural eyes. Thank you, Lord. Amen.

1. Psalm 37:23 AMPC

2. Genesis 1:26a KJV

3. Jeremiah 29:11a AMPC

4. Hebrews 10:23 AMPC

5. 1 Samuel 17:34-37 KJV

_____

_____

_____

_____

_____

_____

_____

_____

_____

_____

_____

_____

_____

_____

_____

_____

From the Back of a Donkey

_____

_____

_____

_____

_____

_____

_____

_____

_____

_____

_____

_____

_____

_____

Chapter Two

———— ⌀ ————

REMEMBERING

Oh my! I must have dozed off! Happens a lot to us pregnant ladies. Sorry! Hmm, where was I? Oh yes, I remember! I've been so busy, getting ready for this trip, and it has been such a long one! But, I was telling you how I was drawing close to God. People have some funny ideas about God and what they think they have to do to please Him. Me, I just think about things and then have conversations with Him about those things.

But, I guess that in itself is unusual, especially for a girl, considering how most folks view us in this time in which I live! My Dad is a bit unusual though. He never once acted disappointed that his eldest was a girl. And he doesn't go for the notion that girls only needed to know cooking and cleaning and sewing and stuff like that. No, I remember him taking me outside to gaze up at the stars while he told me about Father Abraham.

"Daughter, look at the stars," he'd say with a sweep of his arm. "It was these same stars that our ancestor Abraham was told to look at and to count if he could."[1]

After Adam and Eve were kicked out of the garden,[2] it was a very long time, you see, until Abraham was approached by Yahweh. He was minding his own business after leaving the land of Ur,[3] when the Lord Jehovah said to him, "Get out! Go away from your lineage and your father's household. Go to a world and a 'way,' that I will show you."[4]

I love how God talks! Even then, God was speaking of Covenant to him, when He spoke of "The Way," as He sent him on the journey of a lifetime, searching for the city, whose Builder and Maker is God. Kind of like the journey that Joseph and myself now find ourselves on. One of trust and faith.[5]

Here I am with child. Not just ANY child, but HIS seed. And now we have been commanded by Caesar Augustus to journey to our place of lineage for taxation.[6]

We don't know what exactly that will entail. Neither did Abraham when he left his lineage to become "the" lineage of God's promised seed: Jesus. Now, I carry God's lineage in me, and I look up at the stars and I am filled with the wonder of His promises foretold.[7]

Mmm, the fire is crackling and so cozy! The lentils were mighty good tonight. You'll have to excuse me for the evening. All day on the donkey has left me very tired. Please come back tomorrow as we journey. I'd be most pleased for your company and to share with you some more of the marvelous things God has done for me. Okay? See you then!

1. What marvelous things has God done for you?

2. What promises has He given you to hold onto? Have you let them slip? Or are you still holding on?

3. What Words has He whispered to you of encouragement? Is it time to re-read them?

4. What demands have been placed on you by situations beyond your control? As you

journey through them, are you able to see God's hand protecting and guiding you?

5. What things have you taken on that do not belong to you? Do you have the courage to let those things go?

Look up at the stars. They are the same ones Abraham and Mary journeyed beneath. Take heart! Your journey is uniquely your own, but you do not go it alone (unless you choose to.) The King of the Universe, who watches over His Word to perform it, is watching over you.

Dear Lord, thank You that You uphold all things by the power of Your Word.[8] Thank You that my journey of faith and trust is no less significant than was Mary's or Abraham's journey. Help me to realize that I, too, carry God's lineage with me everywhere I go, because I AM now part of that lineage, thanks to Jesus Christ and His birth, death, and resurrection.

Help me to draw close to You in little ways and big ones, that through those moments of intimacy, I, too, may be overshadowed and my life changed day-to-day by Your Glory. Amen.

1. Genesis 15:5 NASB

2. Genesis 3:23-24 KJV

3. Genesis 11:31-32, Acts 7:3 KJV

4. Genesis 12:1-3 NASB

5. Hebrews 11:8-10 KJV, AMPC
   See also NLT for an alternate translation

6. Luke 2:1-6 KJV

7. Genesis 3:15, Gen. 12:3

8. Hebrews 1:3 KJV

Chapter Three

—— ✐ ——

THAT DAY

Oh, hello! I am so glad you caught up with us today. It's nice to have someone to chat with on this trip, it helps to pass the time, which seems to be going so slowly! I have been most uncomfortable on this donkey today. Bless Joseph, he has been patient with my many requests to stop, but finally he said, "Mary, do you want to have this baby right here on the road? We have got to keep moving, so I can find you a proper place!" So I have tried to be a better traveler, although all the bouncing and jostling and the weight of the baby just makes it so hard to not have to stop, if you know what I mean!

I have been thinking about what to share with you next. Let me share "that day" with you. The day the Angel appeared. I'd been busy weaving for Mama. I had taken a moment to get up and stretch my legs and was looking out the window.

And just like that, he appeared!

"Hello Mary, full of grace and highly favored, and approved of God. The Lord said to tell you that He is with you! Blessed, consecrated, set apart, and celebrated are you, forever among women,"[1] he called to me.

Why moments before I had been contemplating my future with Joseph, and Rabbi's message during the last Shabbat, and what Mama wanted to fix for supper that night … Now the whole room was lit up with a bright glow! I rubbed my eyes and wondered if I was daydreaming!

45

"Highly favored? Blessed among and above all women?" What had I ever done to cause me to stand out over and above all women? Although every morning I would wake up and say, "Hear O Israel, the Lord Our God is One Lord. This day Lord I shall love You with all my heart and all my soul and all my might.[2] And, if You grace me to bear Joseph's children, I will teach them Your statutes and speak of Your goodness to them, all the days of my life. Help me this day to please You Lord, and please preserve my life before You. Amen."[3]

Now my poor heart felt like it would jump right out of my chest, it was beating so wildly with fear! Gabriel must have sensed my dismay at his appearance for he quickly said to me: "Do not be afraid, Mary, for you have found grace; free, spontaneous, absolute favor and loving kindness with God." ME! But, his next words left my head spinning and my whole body electrified and giddy. "Behold, you will conceive in thy womb, and bring forth a son, and you shall call his name JESUS."[4]

"But, I'm not married! How? And what about …?" And then, I remembered! A VIRGIN shall conceive and bear a SON … Prophet Isaiah had foretold it.[5] "Was I to be THAT virgin?" Gabriel assured me that "Yes, I was to be that very one!" I could not comprehend how this would be.

Nevertheless, he spoke very confidently and kindly to me. "The Holy Spirit shall come upon you." "You mean that same Spirit that came upon Prophet Isaiah to prophesy of our Messiah's coming?" I asked. "Yes, he said, that same Spirit! Moreover, the Power of the Most High shall overshadow you like a shining cloud."[6]

"Gabriel," I asked, "you mean just like when God spoke 'Light BE', in the beginning and it was and is even to now?"[7]

"Yes Mary, that power, that creation ability, that 'Force' of gathering atoms and molecules and speaking into existence something that had not yet existed. Oh God exists, but now He shall exist as a God-Man and you most favored one are the one that shall carry this Holy Seed and bring it to birth!"

At that point, I pitched forward onto my knees and began to weep and praise God. "Lord, let it be unto me even as Your messenger Gabriel has spoken it."[8]

Suddenly, I was totally cocooned, wrapped in warmth and an energy of luminescent light, which sparkled and danced, swirling about me.

My entire being felt alive, as I have never felt before! It was as if I had not lived, really lived, until this very moment. I know that probably doesn't make any sense, but I don't know how else to explain the feeling that was happening to me and within me. The light touched my skin in wispy brushes, and I tingled. There was such a deep peace, joy, and breathtaking awesomeness as God's very Presence kept enveloping me. I felt as though I was drowning in a sea of Love! The Almighty came to me and claimed me as His! Ahhh. He is so wonderful indeed!

Oh, I can tell by the look on your face that you find my story hard to believe! That's okay, so did Joseph at first. I'll tell you about that later on, okay?

We are nearing our stopping point, and I will need to prepare us something to eat. Would you like to stay and have a meal with us? It won't be anything fancy, just lentils, bread, and dried fish, but you're most welcome you know! No? Okay then, talk to you tomorrow. Shalom.

1. What things has God spoken or shown to you that you are you having a "hard time swallowing?" Why?

2. What is God bringing to you in the way of honour and blessings?

3. How may they or have they changed your life? Are you ready to accept those changes?

4. Write Him an honest letter telling all your fears, concerns, and dreams. Listen for Him to speak back to you.

Dear Lord, I give You permission to divinely interrupt my life and show Yourself strong on my behalf. I say even as Moses said, "Show me Your Glory, Lord!"[9] Help me to make any adjustments necessary to make room for Your Glory in my life. I desire You most of all. Thank You for showing up even in the mundane and chaotic parts of my life. I give You first place, have Your way with me. In Jesus' name. Amen.

1. Luke 1:28-29 AMPC

2. Deuteronomy 6:4-5 KJV

3. Deuteronomy 6:6-7 AMPC

4. Luke 1:30-33 AMPC

5. Deuteronomy 7:14 KJV

6. Luke 1: 34-35 AMPC

7. Genesis 1:3 DRC Douay-Rheims Challoner 1610 AD, KJV, Hebrew H1961 Brown-Driver-Briggs Definition: 1a3: to be

8. Luke 1:38

9. Exodus 33:18 KJV

Chapter Four

———— ☙ ————

AFTERWARDS

Hello again. Nice to see you today. I trust that you rested well and the night passed peacefully for you.

I hope this will be the last day on the donkey! We just have to make Bethlehem soon, please Lord!

Thanks for coming around. I promised to tell you the next part of my story, so here goes:

I don't know how long I worshiped in God's Presence that day. Everything seemed to fade around me. When I finally got up from the floor, the sun was slanting toward afternoon, where it had once been a bright, sunny morning! Gabriel was gone, and the effervescent light that had filled the room was also gone. But what remained was a warm, soft glow inside of me. I knew that God had touched me in a very deep and real way.

Half aloud, half to myself, I exclaimed, "I'll have to hurry now to finish my chores on time." I surely didn't want a bunch of questions about what I had been doing all day! How could I explain this morning to anyone? I'm not sure they would even believe me! Then the thought came: "Elizabeth! She would believe me! If there was anyone on the face of this Earth that would understand this divine encounter, it would be Cousin Elizabeth." Just the mention of her name flooded my mind with pictures of her face and kindness.

I could go under the guise of helping her during this time of her blessed pregnancy.

No one would suspect anything of my going to visit for such a momentous occasion! Maybe she can help me figure out how to tell Joseph. And to share with me what to expect in my coming months … "Yes, I will go visit Elizabeth."[1]

I was beside myself with excitement, and yet this unspeakable peace and joy seemed to bubble within me and buoy me up. I floated through the rest of the day as if encapsulated in God's goodness. I wanted to hug each moment tightly to my heart and savor this heightened awareness of God. I kept rehearsing everything over and over in my mind so as to not forget a single thing of this most wondrous day. Somehow, I finished all my chores in good time. Even that was amazing. Surely, the Almighty had "buttered my steps" to glide effortlessly through my chores![2]

1. Have you ever been overwhelmed by God's Presence? Think about those times.

2. Write them down in as much detail as you can recall. Stretch to remember the littlest things.

3. Now ask God to reveal what you didn't see or remember. To show you what you do not yet know.[3]

4. Get ready to write! He delights in revealing Himself to you and His Plans for you.

Thank You, Lord, for revealing intimate details that only You can know. Thank You for sharing pieces of your heart, even as I share pieces of my own with You.

1. Luke 1:39 AMPC

2. Job 29:6 NASB

3. Jeremiah 3:33 AMPC, DRC

_____

_____

_____

_____

_____

_____

_____

_____

_____

_____

_____

_____

_____

_____

_____

_____

Chapter Five

―――――⸜ᴓᴗ⸝―――――

PREPARING TO GO
VISIT COUSIN ELIZABETH

Hmm, I must prepare quickly, but well. I will need to take some food for the journey there …

Let's see, some bread and cheese, dried fish, olives, apples, figs, and raisin cakes. Several pouches of water.

Oh! I hope that Mama still has that lovely woven blanket as a gift for Cousin Elizabeth!

I wonder what else Mama and Abba will want to send as gifts to cousin Elizabeth and Zachariah to celebrate the baby? Depending on how much they send, I may need to take two donkeys! I'll ride Misha, she will carry me nicely.

I'll need a sack to put my clothes in and another one for the food stuffs and some rope to tie them with … Oh! I mustn't forget my prayer shawl!

Of course, I'll have to convince Abba and Mama to let me go! But it's such a joyous announcement, and I really need to see her, especially now!

I'm sure there is a caravan leaving any day now for Hebron, and from there I can get to the village.[1] I can hardly wait to see Cousin Elizabeth!

That night I told Mother, "I heard some fabulous news today! A messenger named Gabriel stopped by to tell me. No, I don't believe you know him, Mother. You'll never guess! Cousin Elizabeth is going to have a baby! God has blessed her in her old age.[2] I am sure she needs help about now, may I go to visit? Abigail and Darius, our household help, can help you here."

Well, Mother and Abba agreed, and I packed some things, and I sent a note to Joseph by way of one of my younger brothers, telling him I was traveling to go help my elder cousin. I've heard it said that "absence makes the heart grow fonder."[3] I pray that will be the case with Joseph, while I am away.

1. What things do you need to trust God with the details of?

2. What plans do you have? Have you consulted God? Ask God for His wisdom and direction, He will surely guide you, just as He kept Mary safe through every part of her journey.

A man's mind plans his way, but the Lord directs his steps and makes them sure.[4]

1. https://www.holyland-pilgrimage.org/ ein- karem- home-of-john-the-baptist- and- place-of-the-visitation and https:// en.wikipedia.org/wiki/Ein_Kerem

2. Luke 1:36

3. The phrase originated in ancient Rome with a poet by the name of Sextus Propertius from 15BC using it in his work "Elegies." Two Sources: theidioms.com and https:// www.phrases.org.uk/

4. Prov. 16:9 AMPC

From the Back of a Donkey

_____

_____

_____

_____

_____

_____

_____

_____

_____

_____

_____

_____

_____

Chapter Six

────── ⌀ ──────

THE TRIP TO ELIZABETH

Father brought Misha and one of our other donkeys around to the front of the house, prepared the two donkeys for travel himself, and made sure everything was secure and then prayed over me. Just as I had thought, they loaded that poor creature with so many goods to take as gifts to Cousin Elizabeth and Cousin Zachariah. Freshly pressed olive oil, new wine, fruit preserves, lamb jerky, apples, tea and wild honey, the list goes on!

Then he took us to the caravan and spoke with the caravan leader that he was to make sure that I would be kept well-protected! Finally, I set off to see Elizabeth.

As I traveled the distance to my cousin's home, I had plenty of time to reflect on all that had occurred.

It still seemed like a dream. The trip was several days, and the road was quite steep and very dangerous in places.[1] Nonetheless, I was confident that this was God's idea and plan for me to be with Elizabeth, and so I spent the time lost in awe of Him.

The caravan leader, escorted me to the village himself.[2] As we drew near to the house, one of the servants saw me and ran to get someone. "It will be so good to see Elizabeth," I thought. "She is such a blessing to our family, and a godly role model." The caravan master quietly took his leave and left me to greet my cousin privately.

All at once there she was! Her face was crinkled and brown from working outside in the garden, providing for the household. Her hair glinted with hints of silvery streaks in it. But, she was smiling broadly and her arms opened wide in greeting.

I called out a greeting to her. What happened next totally stunned me, although I guess I should be getting used to God's surprises! She clutched her rounded and protruding stomach and then looked up to Heaven. With tears streaming down her face, she looked back to me and began to prophesy in song by the Holy Spirit!

"How exceedingly blessed are you Mary above all women, for you are highly favored of God, and blessed even more, is the baby in your womb. What distinction have I, that I am so honored that you dear girl, the Mother of my Lord, should visit me? Upon hearing your voice, my own child has skipped like a lamb in frolic, leaping in joy, as we see them do when

67

they are let loose from the stall. Oh blessed woman of God, you who dared to believe that what God said, would truly be so! For now, it has come to pass; the fulfillment of what God spoke in those days from long ago. He has given the promise to you to bear and bring forth!"[3]

Now mind you, all I had said up to now was, "Grace and peace be to you my dear cousin …" But, at this juncture, I was so caught up in the moment, I offered up my own song of praise and thanksgiving:

"My soul must magnify the Lord and my spirit is whirling and dancing within me in excitement and rejoicing! Great is the Lord, and I find unspeakable joy and gladness in God, my Savior. Everyone will know how highly He has favored and blessed me! He is mighty in power and mighty must be my praise, for He has done great things and Holy is His Name!"[4]

My thoughts were all a swirl, "Holy Spirit blabbed my secret to her, before I even got to say anything! Wow, I wonder if He will also tell Joseph before I do?" However, there was no time to think any further, because Elizabeth was hugging me, and we were laughing and crying and dancing for joy.

Elizabeth and I had the best time together. We talked and talked, sharing and rejoicing in God together.

Day by day, it became more evident that I really was with child, as the morning nausea set in, and the tiredness would sometimes come at the most inopportune times, but mostly in the afternoons. Elizabeth had the servant girls bring me ginger tea in the morning to help with the nausea, and encouraged me to also take nice long naps with her, whenever she did. Because she requested that I retire in the afternoon with her, everyone assumed that I was taking care of her, so no one questioned me. In fact, we looked after each other, and we knew that God watched over both of us.

Finally, Elizabeth safely delivered her beautiful gift from God, a baby boy, whom they named John. I'm awestruck by this child, for so many reasons. He is, first of all, a miracle. Definitely sent by God with a call upon him. He recognized the gift from God that I am carrying inside of me, while he was yet in his mother's womb! It is more than I can comprehend, I must ponder this in my heart.

The naming of a child is to be given by the father, as is tradition.[5] And then, they take the child to the temple to be presented and a sacrifice brought to honor God. Except my cousin was mute and had been throughout the entire pregnancy! Now, thankfully, after Zachariah had written on papyrus what the name of the boy was to be, then suddenly he could speak.[6] Excitedly, he explained in detail how an angel named Gabriel (my Gabriel!) visited him in the temple and how he had been struck mute until the birth, because he failed to believe the good news that the angel brought to him![7]

He could not stop praising and thanking God, as all of us who had gathered there were also doing. Although my dear cousins and I had very personal reasons to thank God!

Shortly thereafter, I could see that Elizabeth had plenty of willing help, and I surmised from all that was happening with me physically, that I needed to get back home before my belly actually began to poke out prominently, like Elizabeth's did before she delivered! Cousin Elizabeth thought I should not ride alone, and Cousin Zachariah insisted on having several of the temple's altar servants escort me back home with a caravan that was going that way. He is so thoughtful like that. God bless them both!

1. Can you think of a time, place, and/or people that God put in your path?

2. What audacious blessings has God given to you?

3. How can you best steward those blessings?

1. https://aleteia.org/2017/01/ 24/biblical-travel-how- far-to-where-and-what-about-the-donkey/

2. https://www.thejesusbible.faith/where-did-zechariah-and-elizabeth-live-ein-kerem/ Also: https://www.biblestudytools.com/ classics/andrews-the-life-of-our-lord-upon-the-earth/part-i/zacharias-and-elisabeth. html

3. Luke 1:40-45 AMPC and Aramaic Bible

4. Luke 1:44 Leaped Strongs Concordance G4640 to skip 4:2 NASB 2020 & AMPC

5. Luke 1:45-49 AMPC

6. https://bible.org/seriespage/3-why-john-was-not- named-little-zach-luke-157-80

7. https://www.jerusalemperspective.com/2342/

From the Back of a Donkey

Chapter Seven

HOME AGAIN AND THE WEDDING

I no sooner arrived home than Joseph came rushing over. "Mary! You stayed away so long! I have missed you! What was so extremely important that you had to go off in such a hurry? Is it my imagination, or is there something different about you? You seem to be glowing!"

I thought to myself, "Oh yes, big changes Joseph! Changes that I hope you are willing to accept and deal with!" I took a deep breath and began. "Yes, there are changes Joseph, but they are wonderful changes! That was very sweet of you to pick up on that. And it was *really* important for me to go. You see my cousin, who had been called barren, was expecting her firstborn! I needed to go be with her... She has now safely delivered a beautiful baby boy, whom they named John, and so I returned a few days after the temple ceremony."[1]

"That's wonderful about your cousin, Mary. But did you have to be gone for almost four whole months?!" he said, reaching to take my hand. I hesitated but then thought, "Come on girl, you can do this."

I gave him my hand and said, "Yes Joseph, those months allowed me some privacy as I had much to think about and needed to adjust to and deal with changes in my body."

"Oh, Mary! You're not sick are you, my love?" he asked, in alarm. I could see the worry all over his face. "Dear Joseph! How I love you," I thought. "Yes and no, sweet Joey." I hadn't used that nickname before, because it was so ... well, "intimate." But what I was about to tell him couldn't be any more intimate! He looked at me, somewhat surprised and puzzled. "I'm not sick, not like you are thinking." I saw him relax visibly. "Oh Lord help me!" I said to myself. "But I did start having morning sickness, and Elizabeth was so helpful, making me ginger tea and ..."

"You had what?" he interrupted, asking with a trembling voice. "We haven't - so how can you have morning sickness? Mary, what have you done and how could you?" he cried out. "I thought you loved me? I thought we had a life together. You're engaged to me!" He was so distraught.

"Please Lord, soothe him, heal his pain. Let him 'hear!' Joseph, it is not what you think. I have not been with any man. Only meeting daily with God. Joseph, you ARE the one I love! But I love God more than anything, Joseph."

"Yes, I know Mary," he said quietly, "that is what drew me to you - your love for God. That is why I am shocked and hurt now. I do not understand."

"Joseph, He has chosen me to be 'The One!' How could I say no to Him? I'm with child by the Holy Spirit's divine power! It is a miracle. I don't fully understand, but I know it's real." And then, I told him everything, even the prophecy about my new little cousin, baby John.

Afterwards, he just sat there with a glazed, blank look on his face. "Why didn't you tell me before now?" he finally asked.

"I didn't know how," I said simply. "I needed to think about it all. And honestly, I wanted to just hug it to my heart, for it is so wonderful and overwhelming. Only you and Elizabeth know about this."

He just looked at me. "But soon everyone will know," he said. "And they will know it's not mine."

"Not it," I said. "He. JESUS. His name is Jesus!"

Joseph sighed very deeply and stood up. "Mary, I've got to go!"

"When will I see you again, Joseph?" "I don't know, Mary. I just don't know." With that he left. I sat there crying and praying.

"God, You know all things from the beginning to the end.[2] You know every twist and turn along the road I must travel. I don't ask You to spare me hardship. But I ask You to be with me in it and bring me through it.

Like King Jehoshaphat of old, my eyes are on You, Lord.[3] Show Yourself strong on my behalf, and that of Your child I am carrying. Let it be well with us. For Your name's sake, I pray. Amen."

Joseph told me later, that he went home, shattered. He still loved me, but he didn't know what to do either. The more he thought about, it seemed the only answer would be to just quietly annul the marriage contract.[4] At least I would be kept safe from a stoning. He went to bed with a heavy heart and fell asleep. He said he was having a fitful night of it, when suddenly an angel came to him in a dream - or was it a dream? He only knew that the words exploded inside of him.

"Joseph," the angel said, "Don't be afraid to get married to Mary. She has told you the truth. She indeed has conceived a son. He is of God, and from the Holy Spirit. He is both God and Man. He shall be called Jesus, for He shall save his people from their sins."[5]

Joseph said he sat up with a start! "What? Did I hear right? A holy child was coming! I am going to be a parent to the Messiah?!" His next thought was, "We must get married right away! I must protect Mary and the child! Hopefully not many people will talk against her and the pregnancy."

Can you imagine? From being devastated, he was now determined to protect me and the baby! Is it any wonder I love him so? Even if he can be a little quirky about stuff sometimes!

He got busy right away planning everything for my eminent arrival into our matrimonial home. The home had to have his father's blessing, before he could come get me.[6] He had been preparing it all along, but now he gave extra time and diligence to make all things ready.

He gave me about a day's warning to prepare for my wedding day, showing up at midnight with some revelers, all carrying torches and making merry noise.[7]

He stormed the house declaring loudly, "I've come to claim my Bride! Mary, my love, come away with me!"

We then went to the wedding ceremony under the Chuppah.[8]

There under the stars and the wedding canopy, Joseph pledged his love, protection, and provision to me. And I pledged my love and faithfulness to him.[9] There was much merry-making and feasting for seven days as is the custom.[10]

I declined to stay up night after night, as I was already feeling tired and needed my rest. So, we put in our appearances and then snuck away together and left the revelers to celebrate.

It was not exactly how we had planned to have the wedding, so suddenly, or to start our life together. However, the most important thing was and is that we love each other, we love God and we love this child of His!

There is nothing that we can give to God, that He will not repay us in ways we cannot imagine! Truly, the benefits of loving obedience to Him far outweighs any discomfort or sacrifices on our part.

I've enjoyed our conversation, but please excuse me now. I need to stop and stretch my legs and find something to snack on, as it is time for a little bit of food. Hope to catch up with you tomorrow!

Thoughts to ponder

1.   What situations are you facing that have you stymied?

2.   Have you taken time to come aside and spend time with Him, so HE may minister to you?

3.   Are you ministering to Him as well?

4.   Will you trust God even with the things that you don't understand, to work out all the details and perfect everything that concerns you?[1]

Lord, Your ways are marvelous in our sight. We thank You for Your hand of care and Your grace for every situation. Thank You for Your unfailing kindness and goodness to us. We bring You our life and trust in You. Teach us Your ways, oh Lord.[2] We want to know You more. Even if knowing You means ridicule or put down, we still want to know You more. Help us to do that Lord. Amen!

1. The LORD will fulfill that which concerns me; your loving kindness, LORD, endures forever. Do not forsake the works of your own hands. Psalm 138:8 New Heart English Bible (KJV says "will perfect")

2. Show me your ways, LORD. Teach me your paths. Guide me in your truth, and teach me, For you are the God of my salvation, I wait for you all day long. Psalm 25: 4-5 New Heart English Bible

1. Luke 1:13-25 NASB 2020 Luke 1: 57-64

2. Isaiah 46:9-10

3. 2 Chronicles 20:12 NASB 2020

4. Matthew 1:18 BSB

5. Matthew 1:18-25 NASB 2020

6. https://www.thetruthstandsforever.com/ancient-jewish-wedding-customs--jesus-christ-his-bride-the-church.html

7. https://free.messianicbible.com/feature/ancient-jewish-wedding-customs-and-yeshuas-second-coming/

8. https://www.myjewishlearning.com/article/chuppah/

    Pictures of different Chuppahs:
    https://www.google.com/

    https://www.officialroyalwedding 2011.org/jewish-wedding-traditions/

9. The Marriage Contract paragraph 16

    https://www.jfedgmw.org/wedding-customs-old-new-reinvented/

10. The Wedding Feast 2nd paragraph

    https://www.redemptionhillmodes
    to.com/blog/post/ancient-jewish-
    marriage-customs-and-jesus-and-
    his-bride

Chapter Eight

―――――∽―――――

MARRIED LIFE

Life settled down a little after the whirlwind wedding, and I can honestly say it was wonderful! The morning sickness finally abated for the most part. Joseph is very gentle and solicitous toward me, and I feel so loved and blessed. Even in the daily routines there is a wedded bliss, because I can feel God's Presence. I especially enjoy when Joseph comes home for lunch. He likes my lamb stew very much. The moments afforded for the midday meal together seem singularly special to me.

I love taking care of the home and cooking. We even have a lovely garden; however, nowadays, I am mainly permitted to go out and sit down to supervise our help, as Joseph is very protective of the baby and me!

Our home is very sturdy and well-built. I can see Joseph's meticulous workmanship details everywhere I look. Kind of like how I see God's handiwork in the flowers and birds singing and the sunsets and the night sky. How marvelous are the works of your hands Lord![1]

Sometimes as I go about my chores, or as I am riding Misha to town for supplies, I think about Gabriel's visit and his words to me, and the wonder of this child growing inside of me. How will He save our people? I can't help but wonder what the future holds for us, especially me and the holy child that I am carrying.

Often, I have wished that Gabriel would "pop in" for a visit. Mentally I rehearsed all the questions that I would ask him. Then I decided to ask God right out loud, as if He were right here beside me. After all, it is written, "I will never leave you."[2] So, I would pour out my heart to God as I went about my day. Then in the evening when we had prayers, I always felt soothed by the reciting of some of the Psalms.

Thus, our life together fell into a lovely pattern of home, prayers, the carpenter shop, meals, chores, gardening, weaving a baby blanket, and synagogue worship, and all of it filled with God and love for each other.

Several months had passed, and my belly was quite round now.

I rarely go into town these days, except to the synagogue for services, but rather send Aviva, the young woman Joseph hired to help me.

True to her name, Aviva brings springtime into a room with her refreshing and happy demeanor.[3]

For all my contemplating and wondering how God was going to do all that He had spoken to me, I was about to experience the remaining fulfillment of all that Gabriel had told me.[4]

Little did I know that something was coming that would disrupt our beautiful life and it would set into motion what had been foretold long ago.[5]

Have you ever carefully planned something, only to have unexpected events arise and maybe even take over? Take heart, and remember the exhortations in His Word:

Proverbs 16: 1 The Living Bible
We can make our plans, but the final outcome is in God's hands.

Proverbs 16:9 New Heart English Bible Man plans his way, but the Lord directs his steps.

Proverbs 16:9 AMPC A man's mind plans his way, but the Lord directs his steps *and* makes them sure.

Psalm 37:23 KJV The steps of a good man are ordered by the Lord: And He delighteth in his way.

Proverbs 20:24 The Message Bible
Since the Lord is directing our steps, why try to understand everything that happens along the way?

Psalm 138:8 The LORD will do everything for me. O LORD, your mercy endures forever. Do not let go of what your hands have made. GW (God's Word)

The LORD will perfect *that which* concerns me… Psalm 138:8a NKJV

Proverbs 3: 5 Lean on, trust in, and be confident in the Lord with all your heart and mind and do not rely on your own insight or understanding.

Remind yourself of past times when God has helped you and be encouraged. He will work in your present situation to bring about the good plans He has for you. Jeremiah 29:11: (various versions)

Take some time to write down your thoughts, prayers and thanksgiving to God.

1. Psalm 139:14 KJV

2. Joshua 1:5

3. https://www.google.com/search?q=
    The+Jewish+name+Aviva+meaning
    &rlz=1C1SQJL_enUS779US779&oq=
    The+Jewish+name+Aviva+meaning
    &aqs=chrome..69i57j33i160l2j33i22
    i29i30j33i15i22i29i30.1722053829j0
    j15&sourceid=chrome&ie=UTF-8

4. Numbers 23:19

5. Micah 5:2, Isaiah 7:14, Isaiah 9:6, Jeremiah 31:22

From the Back of a Donkey

_____

_____

_____

_____

_____

_____

_____

_____

_____

_____

_____

_____

_____

_____

Chapter Nine

JOURNEY TO BETHLEHEM

Coming into my ninth month, I sent Aviva to town for some honey and a few other things. Imagine my dismay when she came back from town quite excited and upset about some announcement that she saw posted by a Roman soldier in the town square. Something about taxes and a census to count everyone. She was talking very fast and sometimes crying. I immediately sent her to the carpenter shop to request Joseph to come at once. I knew that he would find out what this is all about and what it meant.

When Aviva returned with my Joseph, I could tell by the look on his face that he must have heard something more than what Aviva was saying. Aviva asked, "May I be excused to go check on my parents?" We said, "Yes, of course." Alone now, Joseph put his arms around me and told me not to worry. I rested my head on his shoulder. He assured me, "I will go see the Rabbi, he will most certainly have the proper information and not a bunch of rumors."

When Joseph returned from seeing the Rabbi, he was very quiet and subdued. He suggested we eat dinner, so we blessed the meal and ate quietly. Afterwards, Joseph said, "Mary, what Aviva had told us is true, but incomplete. There are more details, and they affect us directly." Then he told me the whole story, and we sat long into the night talking and praying. Then we recited Scripture.

One piece from King David resonated with both of us:

[By David.] To you, LORD, do I lift up my soul. My God, I have trusted in you. Do not let me be shamed. Do not let my enemies triumph over me. Yes, no one who waits for you shall be shamed. They shall be shamed who deal treacherously without cause. Show me your ways, LORD. Teach me your paths. Guide me in your truth, and teach me, For you are the God of my salvation, I wait for you all day long.[1]

The next morning, we were both up earlier than usual, although very tired. It had been a fitful and restless night with so much to absorb and so many thoughts going through our minds.

Plus, getting comfortable with my big belly isn't always easy! However, we finally reminded ourselves of God's promise to keep us in perfect peace as we keep our heart and mind fixed and focused on Him.[2]

There were so many things to do and a lot to plan for our immediate departure. You see, the announcement that Aviva saw told the news of the census.

The Rabbi filled Joseph in on the details that he had gleaned from the palace. The Roman emperor, Caesar Augustus, ordered that a census (the very first one, mind you!) should be taken throughout his entire empire. Of course, this was mandatory and with no thought to how much this would uproot families and inconvenience everyone. Additionally, it was to commence immediately![3]

Thankfully, both Joseph and I are direct descendants of King David,[4] so we are both required to register in Bethlehem, which is the ancient home of King David.[5] I could not even imagine if I had to go to a different location to register. The very thought of that makes me feel faint!

We made a list of what we needed to do: Joseph will shutter the carpenter shop and close up the house against thieves. I was in charge of compiling enough food for at least ten days of travel[6] due to the uncertainty of how fast we can actually go with me being heavy with child, not to mention the congestion on the roads with so many people traveling to their various destinations.[7]

I went to see my parents before we left. They, too, had to go to Bethlehem and had their own household to deal with getting ready. I kissed them, and we wished each other Shalom - God's unbroken peace.[8] We left ahead of them, but I suspect they may arrive before us, since I seem to need to stop so frequently![9]

I've met so many interesting people on this trip of ninety-plus miles![10] And I've enjoyed your company, I really have. Nonetheless, I will be so glad to reach Bethlehem!

I know Misha will be happy, too! She truly is a Godsend. She has patiently carried me all this way, except when I just had to get down and walk some of the way to stretch a little bit. God bless Joseph, too, for his patience and forbearance.

Surely we must be getting close, don't you think so?

Oh, look! I see lights of a town up ahead! Is it? Yes! It's Bethlehem! I see you in the distance now! Thank you, God! It won't be long! We will be there soon. Oh, I wonder how long this census thing will take anyway. And how long we will be here?

Ouch! What was that twinge? Ohh! There is another one! I must have sat too long, or else sat funny, for there are pains in my back and sides. I will be glad to get into town and settled into a nice room.

A bath sounds so good! And stretching out on a nice bed, to get these kinks out of my back and side.

I hope that we can see each other again. Perhaps get a room nearby one another! I am so glad this donkey journey is almost at an end, but I can't help feeling a whole different kind of journey is just getting started...

Thoughts to ponder:

1. While you are waiting on fulfillment of things promised, here are some Scriptures to strengthen and encourage you:

God is not a man, that he should lie, nor the son of man, that he should repent. Has he said, and will he not do it? Or has he spoken, and will he not make it good? Numbers 23:19 New Heart English Bible

And let us grasp firmly the confession of our hope and not waver, for he who has promised us is faithful. Hebrews 10:23 Aramaic Bible

Do not, therefore, fling away your [fearless] confidence, for it carries a great and glorious compensation of reward. Hebrews 10:35 AMPC

Praising Him in the middle of the wait is very honoring to Him and energizing and uplifting to your spirit!

2. Are there situations that seem to be a huge mountain in front of you?

Call on Jehovah Perez, for God is not only God of our Salvation, but as shown by the revelation of this name, He is also God of our breakthroughs!

So Israel came up to Baal-perazim, and David smote [the Philistines] there. Then David said, "God has broken my enemies by my hand, like the bursting forth of waters." Therefore they named that place Baal-perazim [Lord of Breaking through.] 1 Chronicles 14:11AMPC

See also 2 Samuel 5:20 AMPC

In all your ways know and acknowledge and recognize Him, And He will make your paths straight *and* smooth [removing obstacles that block your way]. Proverbs 3:6 AMP 2015

In all your ways acknowledge Him, And He shall direct your paths. Proverbs 3:6 NKJV

3. Are you stepping out in Faith to follow Him, but are unsure of your next step and don't want to miss Him?

Commit thy works unto the LORD, and thy thoughts shall be established. Proverbs 16:3 KJV

Confusion is not from God. He is never confused, nor does He bring confusion. Jesus tells us that HE IS "The Way." (John 14:6) Follow His leading, and He will lead you in right paths. (Paths of righteousness for His name's sake.) Psalm 23:3

Commit your works to the LORD [submit and trust them to Him], And your plans will succeed [if you respond to His will and guidance]. Proverbs 16:3 AMPC

If you need wisdom, ask our generous God, and he will give it to you. He will not rebuke you for asking. James 1:5 NLT

Throw the whole of your anxiety upon Him, because He Himself cares for you. 1Peter 5:7 Weymouth

Cast your burden on the LORD [release it] and He will sustain *and* uphold you; He will never allow the righteous to be shaken (slip, fall, fail). Psalm 55:22 AMP 2015

Thankfully, we have "the rest of the Book!" Mary only had the Old Testament at the time of her encounter with God. Now, we can learn from her and all the New Testament Saints, as well as Jesus Himself, through the words that have been so carefully recorded for us.

1. Psalm 25:1-5 New Heart English Bible

2. Isaiah 26:3 Amp 2015

3. Luke2:1-2 KJV

4. Luke 3:23-38 (Mary's lineage) see also Luke 1:32, NLT

    https://www.gotquestions.org/Mary-lineage.html

    Matthew 1:1-16 KJV (Joseph's Lineage) and also see the NLT

    Bethlehem Birthplace of King David: https://en.wikipedia.org/wiki/Jesse_(biblical_figure)

5. Luke 2:4-5 AMPC see also: https://gentlereformation.com/2021/12/17/o-little-town-of-bethlehem/

6. https://www.stcatherinercc.org/single-post/2017/12/06/how-long-is-the-trip-from-nazareth-to-bethlehem

    https://www.artzabox.com/a/answers/travelling/traveling-in-israel-distance-from-nazareth-to-bethlehem

    https://www.latimes.com/archives/la-xpm-1995-12-23-me-17102 story.html#:~:text=They%20had%20to%20travel%2090,Jerusalem%2C%20and%20on%20into%20Bethlehem

7. https://blog.adw.org/2014/07/what-was-the-climate-and-weather-of-israel-like-at-the-time-of-jesus/

8. https://firmisrael.org/learn/the-meaning-of-shalom/

    Shalom: Hebrew #7965 Pg. 841 Harmonious relationships between men, Wholeness, Greek Eirene, sometimes Soteria - salvation W.E.Vines expository Dictionary pg.842

9. https://stories.gordon.edu/5-things-you-didnt-know-about-the-christmas-story/

10. https://christianhistoryinstitute.org/magazine/article/on-the-road

11. Map of Israel in Jesus' Time with possible route that Mary and Joseph traveled along the Jordan Valley and River. Annotation by author.

Scripture:

And there were shepherds residing in the fields nearby, keeping watch over their flocks by night. Just then an angel of the Lord stood before them, and the glory of the Lord shone around them, and they were terrified.

But the angel said to them, "Do not be afraid! For behold, I bring you good news of great joy that will be for all the people: Today in the city of David a Savior has been born to you. He is Christ the Lord! And this will be a sign to you: You will find a baby wrapped in swaddling cloths and lying in a manger."

And suddenly there appeared with the angel a great multitude of the heavenly host, praising God and saying:

"Glory to God in the highest, and on earth peace to men on whom His favor rests!"

When the angels had left them and gone into heaven, the shepherds said to one another, "Let us go to Bethlehem and see this thing that has happened, which the Lord has made known to us."

So they hurried off and found Mary and Joseph and the Baby, who was lying in the manger.

After they had seen the Child, they spread the message they had received about Him. And all who heard it were amazed at what the shepherds said to them.

But Mary treasured up all these things and pondered them in her heart.

The shepherds returned, glorifying and praising God for all they had heard and seen, which was just as the angel had told them.

Luke 2: 8-20 Berean Study Bible

Chapter Ten

---- ❧ ----

FROM A MANGER IN BETHLEHEM

Oh, hello! You found me! But how? Oh yes, the star! Of course. Brilliant isn't it? My secret is no longer a secret!

Shhh. You'll have to pardon my whispering, but He is asleep in the manger, and I don't want to awaken him. After we parted last night, the pains intensified and it was then that I knew it was more than a stitch in my side. Joseph was desperate to find us a place to stay and led us from inn to inn inquiring for a room. It was the same everywhere. "No room. Full up." I watched his face, and I saw the concern, the frustration, and the shame trying to take hold of him. "Joseph," I called to him. "Please, don't be hard on yourself. If I hadn't made us stop so many times on the road … Don't blame yourself. God sees you are trying, and you and He have taken such good care of us all the way. His ear is not deaf nor His hand shortened..."[1] At that Joseph brightened and said, "You are right Mary, my brave and beautiful wife! Let's pray."

So, we prayed and asked the Lord for His provision and the place that He would have us to stay and await the birth of Jesus. Joseph went to one more inn and though it was full, the keeper was kindly.[2]

He said, "You young folks should have arrived sooner, you know." Joseph answered, "Yes, sir, I know! But, have you ever traveled with a woman laden with child?

Even now her pains are upon her!"

"What's this?" The innkeeper exclaimed. "We must do something about that. Let me fetch my servant girl, she will take you around back, I have a stable there. It isn't much, but it is private, and sheltered. She will help you get situated."

And so, that is how we came to be here. This is a lovely stable. It is the innkeeper's private stable, where he keeps his own animals.

It is away from the open courtyard and the public stables where many travelers put their stock. It is as most stables go. One side for tethering the animals, and the other side for storing the hay and feed for them. Joseph helped the servant girl to mound a bunch of the sweet smelling hay and put down a blanket for me to lie on. The pains were coming much more strongly, and I wished my mother or Cousin Elizabeth could be here to guide me and help during this delicate "woman's time."

"AAAHHH! OWWWW. OOOOHHH! How long? Lord! Help me! I am afraid!"

Suddenly I heard the words of King David; "What time I am afraid, I will trust in You."[3]

"Oh Lord, I put my trust in You. Help me!"

Now I could hear God reminding me of the words of the Prophet Isaiah: "Fear not! There is nothing to fear, for I am with you; do not look around you in terror and be dismayed for I am your God. I will strengthen you and harden you to difficulties, yes I will help you, yes, I will hold you up and retain you with MY victorious right hand of righteousness and justice."[4]

Oh Lord! You are so good to me! Thank You! I need Your strength. I need Your hand to hold me, I need Your power to endure and prevail. I've never been this way before …

"I know Mary, but when you said yes to ME that day back by the weaving loom, and you allowed ME to overshadow you, did you think I would then leave you to fend for yourself? I WILL bring you through, every step of the way. You are not alone! I will not leave you.[5] Your life and times are in MY hands. I am well pleased, Mary, that you have trusted me even up to this day, though it has not always been easy. There will be times again that will be hard for you.[6] Always remember, I AM with you! Let not your heart be troubled, neither let it be afraid."[7]

The Lord made my delivery lively and quick, just like that of the Hebrew women of old, when Moses was born![8]

May the God of Abraham, Isaac, and Jacob bless my dear Joseph! Men are not usually around during the woman's darkest time, as that is for the womenfolk to see to and deal with. The innkeeper's house girl brought hot water and also some cool water for me to drink. But, after that it was just me and Joseph and God in this little stable last night.

Until the miracle happened. What miracle you ask? Why, the miracle of when HE was born, of course! Isn't He the most beautiful baby in the whole world? His name is JESUS. Yes, I know I told you that earlier, but there is something about that name. I just want to keep saying it, over and over. It's like honey on my lips.

Well, after that it got quite lively around here!

He was born, and then suddenly the whole stable lit up in light. Gabriel appeared to me once again, but this time with a contingency of other angels shouting praises to the Holy and Anointed One, and singing glories unto God!

'Yea, Lord, we greet Thee, Born this happy morning; Jesus, to Thee be glory given; Word of the Father, Now in flesh appearing;[9] O come, let us adore Him, O come, let us adore Him, O Come, let us adore Him, Christ the Lord.'[10]

The Glory of the Lord in the Stable

Then he spoke to me and said, "Greetings beloved of God. Blessed are you among women and so highly favored, Mary. For the Lord who knows you, and called you by name, has kept you and brought you to this day. Now look, you have brought forth the 'Son of His Promise!' He has sent me to announce Him, who shall save His people. But first, I had to come here and see the Ancient of Days clothed in humanity! And to check on you daughter of the Most High..." You are very special to all of us, but more so to God Himself, for He loves you dearly.

With that, he was gone. But, the angel song stirred up the whole stable, and all the creatures were making a racket, like they, too, were singing praises unto God! It was such a sight and noise indeed!

Next, shepherds came running in a short time later, saying they had seen an angel with a choir of angels who announced the birth of the Savior!

I absolutely knew who that angel was! They said the heavenly choir filled the sky with angelic singing. Well, they had certainly filled this little stable with as many as they could squeeze in! I couldn't imagine how many must have filled the sky! Yes, it was quite an eventful night! God announced what He had told me in secret. What I had carried all this time: "The Savior of the World, Emmanuel, God with Us! But now HE is here! And nothing will ever be the same!"[11]

You must excuse me now. I really need some sleep! Please come again when he is awake, to see him, okay? You will want to hold Him close to your heart, and gaze at Him in awe and wonder. I know I do!

As you go, I speak The Blessing over you: "May the Lord bless you and watch over you, guard and keep you; the Lord make His Face to shine upon you, be gracious, kind and merciful to you, giving you favor; The Lord smile upon you and give you peace."[12]

1. When times are hard, do you ask why, or do you press in to Him as never before?

2. When you wish people were there with you and they aren't, and things are not going the way you would choose and desire for them to, do you shut down, or stand up?

3. Do disappointments leave you wondering if you are abandoned, or do you yet believe He loves you and that His hand IS upon you for good? Do you trust Him, even when everyone/everything seems silent, or worse, against you?

4. Remember, God is with you! How can you share this wonderful message? Look for creative ways. (You could even buy a copy of this book to give to someone, if you are unsure how to approach them, and let them hear it from Mary.)

5. Application: Why don't you write out a letter expressing your love and joy in God, as well as any hurts and disappointments? Then search the Scriptures for one or two Scripture promises that covers each situation, releasing those areas to him and expressing trust in His Word to work out everything that pertains to and concerns you.[13]

Thank You, Lord, that You know the beginning from the end. That nothing takes You by surprise.

Thank You that You never leave us or forsake us! Thank You for being the friend that sticks closer than a brother.[14]

Lord, You know my downsitting: when I am depressed and discouraged. And my uprising, whether it is easy for me to get up and praise You, or hard, still I will arise. You know every word in my heart before it ever leaves my tongue![15]

Thank You, Jesus, for leaving Heaven and coming to Earth. Thank You for making that sacrifice to come to Earth, to redeem us back to God. Thank You for granting me the privilege of carrying You in my heart and to other people. Jesus, I DO adore you.

May You always find room in this heart of mine. Amen.

1. Isaiah 59:1 AMPC

2. Luke 2:8-20

3. Psalm 56:3

4. Isaiah 41:10 AMPC

5. Deuteronomy 31:8 Berean Study Bible (BSB) Joshua 1:5

6. Isaiah 43:2 AMPC

7. John 14:1a

8. Exodus 1:19 KJV, AMPC

9. Isaiah 9:6-7 KJV, John 1:14 KJV

10. *O Come, All Ye Faithful - Version* (hymnsandcarolsofchristmas.com) https://hymnary.org/text/o_come_all_ye_faithful_joyful_and_triump

11. Isaiah 7:17, 9:6, Matt. 1:22 AMPC. KJV

12. Numbers 6:24-26 AMPC

13. Psalm 138:8

14. Proverbs 18:24b

15. Psalm 139:1-19 AMPC

From the Back of a Donkey

NOTE FROM THE AUTHOR

I hope you have enjoyed Mary's rendition of the account of Jesus' birth. I pray that you have some God adventures of your own; maybe not as wild as Mary's, but still a definite intersection with the Living God.

If you do not have a personal and growing relationship with Jesus, Father God, and the Holy Spirit, (the Trinity), or maybe you vaguely know about them, but not in a personal way, I urge you to open your heart and invite Jesus to come in as Lord and Savior. After all that is *why* He came! Or, if you do know Him, but want to know Him more, then just ask Him to reveal more of Himself to you and thank Him for hearing your heart's desire.

Prayer is not a religious exercise, but a conversation from your heart to His, and His back to you. So right now, make a conscious decision, and open your mouth and confess that like all of us, you are lost without Him. Ask Him to come into your heart, forgive you, and wipe away all the pain, hurt, and confusion. Give Him permission to work in your life and on your behalf, and thank Him for coming into your heart and bringing you new life.

It really is that simple (although life is not simple for most of us). He makes it easy to approach Him for help, comfort, wisdom, guidance, etc.

So now, believe and expect to find God showing up in your life, because He really loves you and wants to do exactly that!

Welcome to your Journey with Him.

Salvation Scriptures AMPC translation:
Romans 3:23-24, Romans 3:24, Romans 6:23, John 3:16, Romans 10:9-10, Acts 16:30-31, John 16:27, Hebrews 4:15-16, James 1:5

Resources for you:
Bible.com, BibleGateway.com, BibleHub.com, and YouBible apps for desktops, mobile phones, and iPads. E-Sword LT for iPhone includes Strong's and BDB Concordances https://biblehub.net/signup.htm#1 (for desktop)

https://www.e-sword.net Has 4 different links to choose

https://www.bible.com/You Version for desktop (YouBible)

ABOUT THE AUTHOR

Nancy is an expressive Christian, always looking for creative ways to share Jesus. She asked Jesus into her heart as a pre-teen, and received the call to missions as a teenager.

She has done prison ministry and street evangelism in several major cities in the US, as well as outreaches on two Indian Reservations stateside.

From there she founded her own non-profit ministry, Heart n Hands, Inc., traveling to and/ or speaking via technology, to eleven countries, bringing the Gospel and often delivering humanitarian aid as well.

Nancy has helped to build a church in Uganda, seed libraries in Ukraine and Uganda, and plant Bible Schools in Africa. In The Gambia she has supported Bible Clubs in schools, as well as hosted her own radio show for over two years.

She has worked in corporate America for twenty years and recently in higher education, all while running her non-profit and being involved in mission work overseas.

She and her husband, Tom, have been married for over forty-five years. Their adopted children and their families (along with many spiritual children) are scattered all over the globe. Getting to spend time with her children in person or over the phone is always a great joy.

She loves worshiping the Lord, sharing the Word, introducing people to Jesus, and fellowshipping with church family.

Besides writing (she has several more books in process), Nancy enjoys loving on her cats, going out to eat and watching detective shows with hubby, spending time with friends, and going for drives in the countryside. Also, she has a passion for photography. You will often find her roadside snapping photos.

She is incorporating some more of her graphic artwork into her next book and contemplating plans for her photography, under the umbrella of her publishing company, Light Bringer Publishing and Studio, LLC.

Nancy is available for speaking engagements for your events. She has spoken to small intimate groups, as well as crowds from 200 to as large as 4500+ people.

You may reach her here:

Website: Authorladygrace.com

Website: http://lightbringerllc.com

instagram.com/lightbringerpublishing

instagram.com/authorladygrace

instagram.com/heartandhands.inc.ministry

facebook.com/LightBringerPublishing

facebook.com/HeartnHandsMinistry

email: nancyladygrace@gmail.com

Nancy visiting good friends on their farm in Southern Delaware. Here she is with their two donkeys, Mr. Louie, on the left, and Miss Thelma, on the right.